> These things I have spoken to you, that my joy
> may remain in you, and that your joy may be full
> John 15:11

UNCHANGEABLE
UNBREAKABLE
UNSTOPPABLE
JOY

Living a life of triumph and joy
BY RANDY D. RICE

Table of Contents

Forward ———————————————————5

Preface ————————————————————11

Introduction—————————————————13

1. "A Shout Of Joy" ———————————————17
2. "Kingdom Of Joy" ——————————————23
3. "The Spirit's Joy" ——————————————27
4. "Believing Is Receiving" ———————————31
5. "Asking & Receiving" ————————————37
6. "Joy In Trials" ————————————————43
7. "The Joy Set Before You" ——————————47
8. "The Manifest Presence Of God" ——————53
9. "The Joy Of Brokenness" ——————————57
10. "The Joy Of Salvation & The Supernatural" ———61
11. "The Joy Of The Whole Earth" ———————69
12. "The Joy Of Jesus" ————————————75
13. "The Revelation Of Joy" —————————81
14. "Joy At The Throne Of God" ———————89

Conclusion —————————————————95

Forward

Three years ago, my husband, John, my daughter, Teresa, and I walked through the doors of LifeChurch West Chester for the first time and I think we instinctively knew we had found our spiritual home. We felt the warmth of God's love, we felt included and cared about, we sensed His presence continually and it wasn't long before we settled in and found places where we could serve the Lord. For me, I felt called to fast and pray for my pastor, my church and for an end time outpouring of the glory of God and an ingathering and harvest of souls.

On May 18th, 2020, I shared with Pastor Randy that during my prayer time I sensed the Lord desiring him to write a book communicating His plan of salvation through intimacy in relationship with Him. I sensed that multitudes both locally and globally would read it and have their lives changed. Since then, I've been praying consistently for this book and am so excited that it is now here! I know that writing this book has challenged and stretched Pastor Randy's faith but I'm so glad for his special effort because this book is outstanding and exceeds all expectations!

This book could not have been written by just anyone. This beautiful work flows from Pastor Randy's apostolic gifting and anointing and his maturity and stature in ministry. It flows from decades of serving the Lord, walking in faith and delving deep into the Word of God. He is a true spiritual father who excels in discipling others in developing their relationship with God.

One truth I've come to know from sitting under his leadership is that understanding is pervasive throughout every aspect of his ministry. It is present in every contact and in every experience. Understanding is thought of as a common entity, but it is an essential ingredient in ministry. My relationship with the Lord is not only surviving but thriving because of the understanding that exists in our spiritual connection. Proverbs 16:22 says that understanding is the wellspring of life. You will find in this book that Pastor Randy has taken very profound and abstract concepts relating to the Lord and made them easy to understand. I believe as you read this book a portal to the wellspring of life will open up as you endeavor to pursue your relationship with the Lord.

One aspect of Pastor Randy being a true spiritual father is that he speaks the truth and teaches pure doctrine. In this book he has presented a well-rounded concept of spiritual joy by including even the most challenging aspects of being in a relationship with the Lord. There is a quote I loved from chapter eight. "Do you want the joy and pleasure the psalmist spoke about? Ask the Holy Spirit to ignite your heart with the Father's love for His Son. Your heart will feast on the fullness of joy found there." Mother Teresa calls this "the joy of loving Jesus". Yes, just as Pastor Randy shares in his book, if we desire a relationship with the Lord, we may face persecution, we may face trials, we may have to sacrifice to serve others, to build His church and to reap the harvest, but praise God in the midst of it all is heartfelt joy!

Another aspect of Pastor Randy being a true spiritual father is the fruit of his own life measures up to what he is exhorting in others. For instance, Pastor Randy has the right to teach us how to develop intimacy with the Lord because it's such a part of his own relationship with Him. This is apparent to anyone who attends pre-service intercession on Sunday mornings and observes him leading us by praying to the Lord as an intimate friend. Pastor Randy also has the right to exhort us to seek the joy of the Lord in trials because it's already prevalent in his own life. I've personally observed him fast with water only, day after day for seven days straight and during that time I only saw the joy of the Lord shine from his countenance and flow from his lips. And as a nurse, whenever I called to check on him and his dad when they were both seriously ill from COVID-19 I never once heard a negative word from him. His reliance upon his faith in the Lord was both evident and inspirational and I know that kind of strength can only be supplied by the joy of the Lord.

Another aspect of Pastor Randy being a true spiritual father is having the Spirit of Prophecy pouring over his life imparting revelation from the heart of the Lord. The following are some of the descriptions of joy from his book which are sweet and rich in wisdom. I've enjoyed being the recipient of his amazing gifting and I know you will too.

"The fruit of the Spirit is joy and I will taste His fruit continually. Your joy fills me, refreshes me, enables me and sustains me."

"Believing God is always the proper posture of the soul. Believing gets the blessing and is the key to opening doors that no man can shut. If you want to access kingdom glory and flourish with the joy of the Lord, start with simply learning to trust and believe the Father in all things."

"The joy of Jesus has divine strength unlike anything else He could ever give you. It empowers you to overcome the things opposing your witness in the world. Joy emboldens the Christ-follower in the most difficult circumstances. It lightens life's burden and lifts the spirit to soar. No matter what the struggle, the joy of the Lord will fill you with hope…"

"The revelation of joy is simple. It is a revelation of intimacy, acceptance, and communion with God."

Another aspect of Pastor Randy being a true spiritual father is his capability of engendering a fathering presence within each ministry experience. For myself, I know that at times maintaining a ministry of fasting and prayer can require stirring up my passion and building myself up in my most holy faith. However, when I was reading chapter four of this book, it was like the Lord was sitting next to me, encouraging me, strengthening me, reassuring me, and giving me guidance. I could feel an impartation of the joy of the Lord empowering my ministry of intercession. I loved reading that my faith carries joyful victory in it. I loved reading that the God of hope who is always with me loves me more than I could ever imagine and that He knows how to fill me with all peace and joy in believing, I loved reading that my directive from Him is to simply, humbly and joyfully believe. I will always be grateful for this experience and these precious words. Pastor Randy is a true spiritual father in every way.

Let me conclude by sharing a short testimony. A few weeks back, I was getting ready to pray for this book and I couldn't sense the flow of the Spirit, so I just sat and waited for the direction of the Lord. Within a few minutes I felt the Lord extend an invitation for me to join all of heaven celebrating the impending completion of this book. There was a festive atmosphere and I felt joy in God's kingdom! I felt so lighthearted and then an upbeat, jubilant song in the Spirit poured forth from me. All of heaven was rejoicing and I was joining in! I can't tell you how that reassured me and increased my faith to believe the Lord will fulfill the plans He has for this treasure He has created through Pastor Randy.

As for you, it is wonderful that you have found your way to this special book. You will be blessed as you read it. Be prepared for a life-changing impartation of joy unspeakable and full of glory!

With sincerity of heart,
- Sherel Lee Hoyer -

Preface

This book was birthed out of one of the darkest times of my life. In November of 2020 I was diagnosed and quarantined with Covid-19 alongside my eighty-nine-year-old Dad who tested positive for Covid-19 on the same day. Without going into a lot of detail about the physical symptoms of nausea, physical weakness, and headaches the real battle was a spiritual one, against the insidious spirit of despondency. If not for the deep abiding presence of Jesus Christ in my life during this time, and the unceasing joy that flowed from Him, despair it seemed, could have easily swallowed me up. I've described the battle this way, it was as if death itself was endeavoring to knock down the door of my soul and devour my life.

Both me and my Dad eventually overcame the devil-virus, with my Dad having to be admitted to the hospital for three days of treatments. I am thankful to God for our recovery and for the doctors and nurses who assisted my Dad's return to health. I will never forget how the Lord walked with me in this dark season of my life and how His joy was a beacon of light and warmth from Heaven to my soul. I trust this book on the joy of the Lord not only deepens your understanding about His joy but empowers you to live in the glorious light of Christ and His victorious joy through every circumstance of your life.

- Pastor Randy D. Rice -

Introduction

"In the world you will have tribulation; but be of good cheer, I have overcome the world."
John 16:33

The Apostle Peter wrote: *"Celebrate with praises the God and Father of our Lord Jesus Christ, who has shown us his extravagant mercy. For his fountain of mercy has given us a new life—we are reborn to experience a living, energetic hope through the resurrection of Jesus Christ from the dead. We are reborn into a perfect inheritance that can never perish, never be defiled, and never diminish. It is promised and preserved forever in the heavenly realm for you! Through our faith, the mighty power of God constantly guards us until our full salvation is ready to be revealed in the last time. May the thought of this cause you to jump for joy, even though lately you've had to put up with the grief of many trials. But these only reveal the sterling core of your faith, which is far more valuable than gold that perishes, for even gold is refined by fire. Your authentic faith will result in even more praise, glory, and honor when Jesus the Anointed One is revealed. You love him passionately although you have not seen him, but through believing in him you are saturated with an ecstatic joy, indescribably sublime and immersed in glory. For you are reaping the harvest of your faith—the full salvation promised you—your souls' victory"* I Peter 1:3-9. (The Passion Translation)

The apostle Peter was not yet imprisoned for his faith when he wrote these words, but the clouds of persecution were gathering. Nero was becoming more erratic and tyrannical toward Christians, and the apostle Peter could see what was on the horizon. It would not only test his faith and devotion to Christ but would test every follower of Christ in the emerging churches throughout the Roman Empire. The Roman political class, along with empire elitists were opposed to the humble, developing Christian communities who worshipped the only true King Jesus instead of Caesar. The age-old conflict between light and darkness was intensifying everywhere, as the gospel of Jesus Christ went forth throughout the realm. Demonic principalities and angelic hosts were warring in the heavenlies making it a triumphant time for the Lord's church and a turbulent time as well.

Stirred and undaunted by what he saw coming, the apostle Peter penned the amazing words that we see above. His epistle to the churches would serve as a powerful signal fire for God's people to prepare their heart and mind for the approaching storm of persecution. He knew that God's people and the fledgling churches would not survive without God's supernatural strength to make it through. He also knew from his own experience that only the overflowing joy of Jesus in their heart would provide the supernatural comfort and strength they would need to overcome the suffering ahead and continue to spread the gospel of Jesus Christ everywhere.

In much the same way, Christians today sense a prophetic foreboding in the land. Clouds of discrimination and harassment against Christians are rising all around the world. Even in the freest of nations of the world ominous, anti-Christian rhetoric continues to rise against believers. Media, academia, and government institutions posture themselves against the Lord's Church with fierce pressure toward Christians to conform to anti-Christ standards or suffer the consequences. Without question, the battle lines between good and evil are becoming more defined and intense. And again, the word of the Lord to His church today amid the darkness is the same word the apostle Peter was inspired to write to the early church. It is the message of the unchangeable, unbreakable, unstoppable, and glorious joy of the Lord.

As you begin to pour over the following pages, I pray the Holy Spirit will do exactly what the apostle Peter wrote about, pour into you His *"indescribably sublime and immersed in glory"* joy. I pray that His joy will awaken in you and propel you forward through any coming persecution, trial, or temptation that you might face, and that this simple book will contribute in some small way to your supernatural strength and power in Christ through it all. I hope it will be something you refer to again and again as you live your life for Christ, and if ever occasion arises that your joy in the Lord dims within you, that you will pick it up again to be refreshed in your spirit by the truths it shares. I pray the ember of joy in you will soon turn into a flame, and the flame will turn into a signal fire for all to see, especially to those whom you love and even those who do not understand the supernatural joy you possess.

It is through you that Jesus has chosen to reveal His joy to the world. Do not be dismayed if there are those who oppose you or do not understand you. Remember, they cannot comprehend the joy of the Lord because they have never received of it, nor tasted of it. It is unimaginable to those who have not experienced it. But to those of us who have known it, nothing in this world can match it! The world did not give it to you, and the world cannot take it from you. When you cultivate joy in your spirit-man, it shines through all you do. The lost will take notice. The skeptic will be curious. The backslider will desire to taste of it again, all because you possessed it and demonstrated it in your walk with God. It truly is unshakable in every battle, unbreakable in every storm, and unstoppable in every crisis. And most of all, it is unchangeable through all time and eternity. It can never be altered by any earthly source, nor diminished by the darkness around you. It comes to you direct from the heart of the Father, Son and Holy Spirit. Open your soul now and receive the infinite joy that Jesus possesses and eagerly gives you. Your soul will find no greater rest and your spirit no greater satisfaction than abiding in His ever-increasing and always satisfying joy. As the apostle Paul said, *"May the God of hope fill you with all joy and peace as you trust in him, so that you may overflow with hope by the power of the Holy Spirit"* – Romans 15:13. (NIV)

CHAPTER 1

"A SHOUT OF JOY"

"Rejoice in the LORD, O you righteous! For praise from the upright is beautiful. Praise the LORD with the harp; Make melody to Him with an instrument of ten strings. Sing to Him a new song; Play skillfully with a shout of joy. For the word of the LORD is right, and all His work is done in truth."
Psalms 33:1-4

With a shout of joy, the walls of Jericho came down. With a shout of joy, a hundred and twenty followers of Christ burst out of the upper room filled with the Holy Spirit. With a shout of joy, the voice of the archangel will sound as the Lord descends from Heaven to rapture His beloved Bride. Shouts of joy prevail over darkness! Shouts of joy are powerful against the enemies of God. They open Heaven and shut down hell. They release angels from on High and bind-up demons below. *Psalm 149 says, "Praise the Lord! Sing to the Lord a new song, and His praise in the assembly of saints. Let Israel rejoice in their Maker; Let the children of Zion be joyful in their King. Let them praise His name with the dance; Let them sing praises to Him with the timbrel and harp. For the Lord takes pleasure in His people; He will beautify the humble with salvation. Let the saints be joyful in glory; Let them sing aloud on their beds. Let the high praises of God be in their mouth, and a two-edged sword in their hand, to execute vengeance on the nations, and punishments on the peoples; To bind their kings with chains, and their nobles with fetters of iron; To execute on them the written judgment– This honor have all His saints. Praise the Lord!"*

The saints of the Lord bind the enemies of the Lord with their high praise. Those who have been washed clean by the blood of Jesus possess spiritual authority over all the enemies of God. Their shouts of joy bind evil principalities. When the righteous raise their praise the heavens and the earth tremble. Their shouts glorify God and break chains of darkness. Their voices are like shafts of light in the spiritual realm releasing the piercing fire of Christ! Demonic strongholds tremble at the sound of it. Their shouts are like God's lightning and thunder against the dark caverns of hell. When the righteous sing with joy to the Lord, they bring honor in God's house and fear to the enemy's camp. When they awake from slumber and shout with joy, they overwhelm their enemies and rout their adversaries. Their declarations of joy move the heart of Almighty God. He defends them and surrounds them with His glory. This is the heritage of the saints of the Lord. This is the privilege of those who know and walk with Him.

The Lord loves when you shout out of love for Him. He delights in your delight of Him. He rejoices in your rejoicing in Him. He makes mountains quake and move at the sound of your praises. Darkness must flee when the children of light lift their voice and sing to Him. Songs of praise are mighty weapons. The Lord has determined it to be so. You are a blessing to Him and a weapon of victorious warfare when you praise Him with a full heart and a loud voice.

Nothing is more pleasant and potent in the spiritual realm than for His saints to glorify Him. Through you God has chosen to bring Heaven to earth and drive demons into the dust. When you praise Him, you rise to new levels of power and anointing in the Spirit. New heights of glory in the Spirit are achieved when you worship with His joy flooding your soul. At the sound of your praises, angels dance, demons flee, and the glory of God's presence returns afresh to dwell among His people. When faced with hopelessness and despair your praise is a powerful weapon. The Apostle Paul and Silas knew that their high praises, even while in prison and chains were a spiritual weapon that demons and dungeons could not withstand.

After being beaten and thrown in jail for preaching the gospel, the apostle Paul and Silas did not hesitate to raise praise in their distress. In the darkest and most miserable place, they prayed and sang hymns to the Lord. While in physical and emotional pain, they lifted songs of praise to God together. Their heavy chains and shackles where no match for their lifted voices and shouts of joy. *"At midnight Paul and Silas were praying and singing hymns to God, and the prisoners were listening to them. Suddenly there was a great earthquake, so that the foundations of the prison were shaken; and immediately all the doors were opened, and everyone's chains were loosed" Acts 16:2-26.* Beloved, you must never forget the power of your praises to God and your songs to Him in the night seasons. There is power from Heaven in your praises! There are chains that you must break and heaviness that you must cast off. When you sing to the Lord with joy in your heart, He inhabits your praise and undoes the heavy burden. He hears your songs in the night and responds to them with His peace and with His power!

Do you feel you cannot sing due to a valley you are in, or a recent rejection you've endured? Do you feel your shouts of praise are not genuine in such times? Or, do you feel awkward when you lift your voice, or somehow your praises are not acceptable to God in your weaknesses? Has the Devil lied to you and told you your shouts of praise and joy are foolish? Has he slyly whispered in your pain, *"What difference will your shouts make considering the situation you are in?"* Do not be fooled, beloved! Do not allow Satan's lie to become your prison of despair! Have faith in God! Rise up and counter his lies with the truth of God's word! Do not permit him to silence you. Be determined and courageous!

Shouts of praise and joy are good and glorious to the Lord, and they are good and right in His sight. Lifting your voice like a trumpet takes effort, energy, and humility. Let all of Heaven hear you, and make sure the devil can't ignore you! Your shouts of joy and praise have authority with God and power over the devil! When you shout for joy and sing to the Lord, you will never fail to walk in victory. His word promises it. Your shouts of joy declare His word of victory for you. Your shouts of joy proclaim that God will never fail you! So, take up a shout to the Lord the next time you feel oppression trying to move in on you. Lift your voice like a trumpet and watch how quickly the oppression moves out and the glory of the Lord moves in! Your voice is a two-edged sword. When you raise it in praise, alignment with God occurs and streams of blessing break forth like mighty rivers. Use your voice! Wield it like the sword of the Lord that it is! Satan will not stay to harass you, and powerful angels of the Lord will come and minister to you!

Declaration of Joy: "Heavenly Father, thank you for my voice! You gave it to me, and I will use it more and more. Forgive me for not lifting it up to You in joyful praise more often. Thank You for the revelation that it is like a two-edged sword when I shout Your word, Your will, and Your praises! I rejoice that shouts of joy from me are gladly received by You! Thank You that Heaven rejoices when I sing and bring praises to You. Hell has no weapon that can prosper when my shouts of praise to You ascend. Every spiritual door is opened, and every chain of darkness is broken when I shout Your praises. Thank You, Heavenly Father that You delight in my praise, and smile when I sing to You. I will not neglect this wonderful blessing! My voice is Your instrument of warfare against my enemies and an instrument of worship to You! Thank You for this wonderful revelation! I will not cease to praise and bring glory to You! In Jesus' mighty and glorious name I pray, Amen!"

CHAPTER 2

"KINGDOM OF JOY"

"For the Kingdom of God is not eating and drinking, but righteousness and peace and joy in the Holy Spirit."
Romans 14:17

Not only is God's kingdom an unshakable dominion of righteousness and of peace, it is also a dominion of complete and everlasting joy. The apostle Paul makes a powerful claim here in Romans 14:17. He says that God's kingdom *"is"* joy! Think about it. *"Is"* is a word that describes the very essence and scope of God's kingdom. God's kingdom not only has joy, but it is comprised of joy. In other words, as a citizen of Heaven you breath it, you feel it, you taste it, and enjoy it. Kingdom joy is in you and all around you. There are no aspects of God's kingdom that have less joy, or more joy. The kingdom of God is joy!

If then the kingdom of God is joy, it begs the question, what is joy? Joy is simply the feeling of good cheer and extreme gladness. It is the intrinsic sense of God's great pleasure and goodness in you. It is created by God and sustained by Him. His joy is supernatural and there is a boundless supply for you. Joy is Heaven's gladness and bliss straight from your Heavenly Father. The kingdom of God is constantly filled and overflowing with it. Whoever enters the kingdom experiences its transforming power. Any repentant sinner through faith in the Lord Jesus Christ receives it. Jesus said, *"I am the door, if anyone enters by Me, he will be saved, and will go in and out and find pasture. The thief does not come except to steal, and to kill, and to destroy. I have come that they may have life, and that they may have it more abundantly" John 10:8-10.* Abundant life in God's kingdom includes abundance of joy.

Paul declared in Acts 20:20-21, *"I kept back nothing that was helpful, but proclaimed it to you, and taught you publicly and from house to house, testifying to Jews, and also to Greeks, repentance toward God and faith toward our Lord Jesus Christ."* When you put your faith in Jesus Christ you became a citizen of Heaven. The Holy Spirit came into your heart and you were born again. Not only are you in the kingdom of God now, but the kingdom of God is in you. Luke 17:21 says, *"Now when He (Jesus) was asked by the Pharisees when the kingdom of God would come, He answered them and said, 'The kingdom of God does not come with observation; Nor will they say, 'See here!' or 'See there!' For indeed, the kingdom of God is within you."* When you arrived in the kingdom and the kingdom arrived in you, for the first time you were able to see, experience, hear, live, and intimately know the King and the kingdom. One of the first and most overwhelming feelings that met you upon entry was the unspeakable, unexplainable joy that fills all of Heaven. Entering God's kingdom opens you up to the unending flow of kingdom joy. Joy is the atmosphere and oxygen of the kingdom of God. His joy never ceases to refresh and renew His people. It empowers them to greater fruitfulness and blessing. Though physical and emotional strength might wane, the joy of the Lord will never wane. It is constant and always accessible for the weary warrior. It is unceasingly moving toward those who humbly wait on the Lord for new strength.

The prophet Isaiah spoke of the kingdom of joy when he wrote, *"Have you not known? Have you not heard? The everlasting God, the LORD, the Creator of the ends of the earth, neither faints nor is weary. His understanding is unsearchable. He gives power to the weak, and to those who have no might He increases strength. Even the youths shall faint and be weary, and the young men shall utterly fall, but those who wait on the LORD shall renew their strength; They shall mount up with wings like eagles, they shall run and not be weary, they shall walk and not faint"* Isaiah 40:28-31. Beloved, I pray your wings of unwavering faith in Jesus Christ cause you to soar in His unending joy. Right now, Jesus invites you to mount up with Him on the wings of joy. He invites you to rise above the storms and ascend in the glories of the Eternal realm. The greater your faith and trust in Him, the greater the joy you experience in Him. You need not ever become faint or grow weary, my friend. The never-ceasing, and ever-flowing joy of the Lord renews your strength! Kingdom joy never abates nor diminishes for those who seek Him.

Declaration of Joy: "Heavenly Father, thank You for the unrelenting joy of Your kingdom. I lift my gaze to You, to Your Eternal Throne, where You sit as King of kings, and Lord of lords. I lift my voice to You and thank You for the ever-flowing river of joy that is mine, through Your Son, Jesus Christ. Thank You, that Your joy is inexhaustible and always accessible to me. In every circumstance, I declare that I receive Your kingdom of joy. Help me to never neglect it, always embrace it, forever live in it, share it, and speak of it to others. I ask it all in the mighty Name of Jesus I pray, Amen!"

CHAPTER 3

"THE SPIRIT'S JOY"

"But the fruit of the Spirit is love, joy, peace, longsuffering, kindness, goodness, faithfulness, gentleness, self-control. Against such there is no law." Galatians 5:22-23

The Holy Spirit's joy is likened unto "fruit" for good reason, it's like a tasty, hearty consumable for the spiritually hungry and physically weary. I know that sounds strange, but let me assure you that when your soul is tested and the heat of battle is long, it's the fruit of the Holy Spirit and predominantly the fruit of joy that will refresh you in the fight. The apostle Paul wrote, *"For we do not wrestle against flesh and blood, but against principalities, against powers, against the rulers of the darkness of this age, against spiritual hosts of wickedness in the heavenly places"* Ephesians 6:12. At any time in any spiritual skirmish, the fruit of joy is yours for the taking. Taste of it in your trials and you will always return for more. It drips with contentment and happiness and fills the weary soul with strength and power.

The psalmist writes, *"Oh, taste and see that the LORD is good; Blessed is the man who trusts in Him"* Psalms 34:8. Like fruit hanging from the branches of a great tree, the fruit of joy hangs from the very essence and presence of the Holy Spirit. *"Taste and you will see"*, the Psalmist writes. Though the battle rages all around you, the Spirit of God offers His fruit of joy to you. Though your trial is hot, you will find rest and refreshing when you taste and see. You only need to turn your soul toward the Lord and partake. When you taste of the Spirit's joy your trials and weariness abate. Have you been tested lately? Has the heat of battle wearied you, good soldier? The Spirit's joy will renew you in warfare and cause the smoke of spiritual combat to drift away. The Psalmist writes, *"For You have armed me with strength for the battle; You have subdued under me those who rose up against me" Psalm 18:39*. The weapons of your warfare are not fleshly weapons, they are spiritual weapons. The Lord has armed you with weapons much more potent than anything Satan can launch at you. The Lord equips and readies you for the good fight of faith. Not with worldly weapons of man's warfare, but with spiritual fruit, the fruit of joy, love, peace and more. He delivers you and refreshes you from the battle with the fruit of the Holy Spirit.

Did you know deliverance is promised to you? Victory is always offered to the child of God. The Father promises to deliver you from every temptation and bring you through every test. The apostle Paul declares, *"No temptation has overtaken you except such as is common to man; but God is faithful, who will not allow you to be tempted beyond what you are able, but with the temptation will also make the way of escape, that you may be able to bear it" I Corinthians 10:13*. The Psalmist affirms, *"No king is saved by the multitude of an army; A mighty man is not delivered by great strength. A horse is a vain hope for safety; Neither shall it deliver any by its great strength. Behold, the eye of the Lord is on those who fear Him, on those who hope in His mercy, to deliver their soul from death, and to keep them alive in famine. Our soul waits for the Lord; He is our help and our shield. For our heart shall rejoice in Him because we have trusted in His holy name. Let Your mercy, O Lord, be upon us, just as we hope in You" Psalm 33:16-22.*

It is the Spirit's joy in you that helps you withstand confrontations with demons and darkness. He brings hope in your hopelessness. He offers the fragrance of confidence in your midnight watches. Your battles are not won with anger and frustration, but rather with the overflowing, life-giving fruit of the Spirit of God within you. He is the source of all love, joy, and peace in every spiritual conquest.

Are you in a battle right now? Quiet your mind. Are you facing a Goliath in front of you? Still your soul, good soldier. The Holy Spirit is with you. He will not leave you in the storm alone and helpless. He will not cease to offer His strength to you. His peace and joy will empower you. Trust him. Touch Him. The Holy Spirit is there with you. Your battle is not with people, or circumstances, it's with the unseen realm of darkness, and your secret weapon is the fruit of joy. Face your enemies with the Spirit's radiance and you will conquer all. No weapon formed against you can prosper when you constantly eat of the fruit of joy, love, and peace. Do not fear, child of God! In every situation, the Spirit's fruit is a fresh taste of victory, a delightsome fragrance of hope, and a mighty weapon of war for you.

Declaration of Joy: "Thank You, Heavenly Father for the Spirit's joy within me. I will turn my heart to Him, and He will flood my soul with joy. When I am dismayed, I will direct my thoughts to be still. Whenever I am alarmed, I will not be confused by the noise. The fruit of the Spirit is joy, and I will taste His fruit continually. Your joy fills me, refreshes me, enables me, and sustains me. No matter how heated the battle Your joy shall equip me for victory. Thank You Father for filling me with the Holy Spirit. I am never alone, I am never outnumbered, and I am never overpowered because of Him in me. I will forever trust in You and will never be put to shame. In the strong and matchless Name of Jesus I pray, amen."

CHAPTER 4

"BELIEVING IS RECEIVING"

"Now may the God of hope fill you with all joy and peace in believing, that you may abound in hope by the power of the Holy Spirit."
Romans 15:13

You have heard it said many times, "seeing is believing". In a world of mistrust, suspicion, and sin, disbelieving is the default response for most people. It makes sense for those in business to feel a measure of mistrust in their fields of expertise. A no-nonsense, verify all things, and leave no stone unturned approach makes sense in the world of business. But, in the kingdom of God, suspicion is not needed. The mistrust of God, and mistrust of God's kingdom is a mistake for those of us who endeavor to live victoriously for Christ.

In the kingdom of God, doubt is detrimental. It delays promotion and hinders advancement. In the kingdom of God, believing is always the path forward. Believing God is always the proper posture of the soul. Believing gets the blessing and is the key to open doors that no man can shut. If you want to access kingdom glory and flourish with the joy of the Lord, start with simply learning to trust and believe the Father in all things. When you do, you find His kingdom to be unshakable, undeniable, and unmovable amid a world of uncertainty and suspicion.

It's difficult for most of us to fully trust anyone when we've been lied to and taken advantage of in the past. Perhaps, the hucksters and liars have been in abundant supply over the years of your life. But, in God's kingdom trusting and believing Him in all things is right and good. Get this principle wrong and you will become spiritually stuck. Believing in God is not only where you start in the kingdom, but believing Him in all things is also how you run the entire race for Christ. Without believing there is no spiritual breakthrough. When you believe God, *all things are possible with God*. The desperate father in Mark 9:23, who brought his tormented son to Jesus heard these powerful words in his darkest hour, *"If you can believe, all things are possible to him who believes"*. When you consistently and humbly believe God, miracles suddenly happen.

Your Heavenly Father loves when you believe Him. He loves when you take Him at His word. He listens intently to your thoughts of certainty in Him and conversations of confidence to others about Him. He hears your prayers of faith, and carefully measures your quiet assurance and unspoken motives too. Your opinions and meditations are important to Him. He knows your frame and your frailty, and when you acknowledge your doubts before Him. He smiles when you press through the weakness you feel and walks beside you as you defeat your inner worry and fear. When no one else can see your faith breaking through your inner man, He can. He looks with delight as your faith breaches the darkness you feel. He knows the countless tears you've cried and how those tears have led you to Him and to faithful intercession before Him. He hears your heartfelt groaning in the Holy Spirit. Your prayers of faith are sweet and precious to Him. He shouts with you as you believe Him for small things and great things alike. He treasures your acts of faith in Him and rejoices over them! When you believe Him in all things, all things become possible in Him.

Believing is always right in His sight. Before you ever see the answer in the natural, believe it is yours already! Before you ever enjoy the fulfillment of your request answered, believe that you receive it! Before you walk in His answer from Heaven, believe Him in your darkest moments and you will receive His blessing. Jesus said, *"Therefore I say to you, whatever things you ask when you pray, believe that you receive them, and you will have them" John 17:8.* Believing is your access to the supernatural things of the kingdom. Believe, and you shall receive the things your Heavenly Father has destined for you.

The psalmist writes, *"But let all those rejoice who put their trust in You; Let them ever shout for joy, because You defend them; Let those also who love Your Name be joyful in You" Psalms 5:11.* The apostle John put it this way, *"Whoever is begotten of God overcomes the world: and this is the victory that hath overcome the world, even our faith" 1 John 5:4.* Faith is the victory that overcomes all that is in the world. Believe God, in all things and in every circumstance, and His joy, hope and power will not cease to flow to you. Believe, and keep believing, and His joy will flood your heart and mind. Beloved, believing is receiving! Kingdom faith has always functioned this way. The book of Hebrews states, *"Without faith it is impossible to please God; for he that comes to God must believe that He is, and that he is a rewarder of them that diligently seek Him"* Hebrews 11:6. The God of all hope loves to fill His children with His joy and peace in believing Him. Just as you abound in faith, you will also abound in joy and peace in Him.

If there are doubts and fears, brush them aside! If there are disappointments and despair, stand in faith in the midst of them! If you make a sudden mistake or wrong decision, believe that God will turn it around for your good and His glory! The bible tells us, *"Likewise the Spirit also helps in our weaknesses. For we do not know what we should pray for as we ought, but the Spirit Himself makes intercession for us with groanings which cannot be uttered. Now He who searches the hearts knows what the mind of the Spirit is, because He makes intercession for the saints according to the will of God. And we know that all things work together for good to those who love God, to those who are the called according to His purpose." Romans 8:26-28.* Your faith carries joyous victory in it. Believe God no matter what the circumstances and He will intervene. The Father loves to turn impossible situations into incredible blessings. But if you give up, the blessings can be delayed or even lost. Nevertheless, when you believe God, He will turn every defeat into triumph and grant freedom from every burden. The God of hope, who is always with you and loves you more than you could ever imagine, knows how to fill you with all joy and peace in believing. And so, your directive from Him is to simply, humbly, and joyfully, believe! Like Jesus said to broken hearted Martha at the graveside of her brother Lazarus, *"Did I not say to you that if you would believe you would see the glory of God?"* So, Jesus says to you, *"Only believe and you shall see the glory of God."*

Declaration of Joy: "Heavenly Father, thank You for teaching me to believe You in everything. I will not avoid my weakness. I will not ignore my doubts and fears. Instead, I will show them to You and ask for your joy and power over them. Thank You, that believing is the bridge to open doors and promotions in Your Kingdom. It is the one way I know You are always pleased with me. I know You always have surprises that spring forth from Your Presence when I live by faith. Let your joy and peace abound in me through the power of Your Holy Spirit. I promise to faithfully trust in You in every victory and in every battle! In the powerful Name of Jesus I pray, Amen!"

CHAPTER 5

"ASKING & RECEIVING"

"And in that day, you will ask Me nothing. Most assuredly, I say to you, whatever you ask the Father in My name He will give you. Until now you have asked nothing in My name. Ask, and you will receive, that your joy may be full."
John 16:23-24

Did you know that your Heavenly Father is a God of conversations? Has anyone ever shared this revelation with you about Him? He is, and He especially loves conversations with you. It's an astonishing thought that you and I can speak to Almighty, Creator God as Friend with friend. When you understand this truth about your Heavenly Father your prayer life will never be the same. Allow me to gently remind you, one of the great reasons Jesus came to us, died on the cross for us, and rose again from the dead to save us was so we could have transformational conversations with our Heavenly Father, just like He did. Your Father enjoys when you talk with Him. He loves to listen as you ask things of Him, and He loves to answer at just the right time. He cares when you're sorting through cumbersome thoughts and concerns. Our cluttered and burdened minds are no match for His brilliance and words of wisdom.

Your Heavenly Father is not like earthly fathers. Earthly fathers are imperfect at best, but your Heavenly Father is wonderful and altogether perfect. Have you experienced rejection from an earthly father in the past? So many precious people have, and so often their wounded hearts hinder them from the beautiful and intimate relationship their Heavenly Father plans for them. Rejection of any kind is painful, but it is especially painful and difficult when it's the very one who is supposed to protect you, provide for you, and encourage you. Fortunately, your Heavenly Father is not a failed earthly father. Without question, there are many outstanding earthly fathers, but none can match the One who is always accessible, always loving, and always with you in every circumstance of life. Think about it! Your Heavenly Father through Jesus Christ made a way for you to commune intimately and personally with Him. Through our Savior Jesus Christ, He broke down every barrier in the natural and spiritual realm so you can have access and friendship with Him. This is the heart of your Heavenly Father. He gave His best to not only save your soul but to win your heart and bring you into eternal, unbroken fellowship with Him.

Face to face conversations with God are what He wants with you. Like a Father and a son or daughter, your Heavenly Father awaits your attention. Like friends who enjoy discussing the happenings of the day, your Heavenly Father enjoys discussing the day with you. Topics of interest are always welcome with your Father in His throne room. Your pain, confusion, failure, or problem can always be discussed without shame, or fear of condemnation from Him. Your Father enjoys fellowship with you, He desires to show you things about yourself and your life that will encourage you, heal you, and replenish your joy in Him.

Asking big things and little things is not an issue with Him at all. He's never stingy with intervention, answers, and help. He always has an abundant supply of strength for you and a world of resources too. He likes to be involved in every detail of your life and the progress of your welfare. Even though you sometimes get distracted by pressures and people, He's never distracted and is forever vigilant toward you. He is always there with His inviting smile to offer grace to you and hear your voice. Your Heavenly Father is a great listener too. Truly, God is the God of dialog. Long conversations, short conversations, and even sitting without a word, conversations. Most conversations we engage in have a start and a finish, but since your Father dwells in eternity, conversations with Him are continual. We may forget most of the conservations we had yesterday, but your Heavenly Father remembers all the details of your conversations with Him, even the thing you didn't say out loud. He wants you to know His conversations with you are eternal and His answers are always good.

As you go through the day, and before you go to sleep at night try talking to God as you would a friend. It's liberating and empowering. Ask Him things, and He will give you answers about them. Your heart will brim full of joy one conversation at a time with Him. The Father knows your thoughts and He desires you to know His too. This is how His joy becomes full and overflowing in your life. Some might argue, what about the words of the prophet Isaiah who wrote, *"For My thoughts are not your thoughts, nor are your ways My ways, says the LORD. For as the heavens are higher than the earth, so are My ways higher than your ways, and My thoughts than your thoughts" Isaiah 55:8-9.*

Nevertheless, we are assured that with Christ in us we can know His thoughts and His ways through the indwelling Spirit of God. The apostle Paul wrote, *"Who has known the mind of the LORD that he may instruct Him? But we have the mind of Christ" I Corinthians 2:16.*

Prayers are much sweeter when you've made specific requests to God. When you pray specific prayers your Heavenly Father will give you precise answers. Answers without friendship and conversation with God can occur, but it will not create the fullness of joy Jesus refers to when He says, *"In that day, you will ask Me nothing. Most assuredly, I say to you, whatever you ask the Father in My name He will give you. Until now you have asked nothing in My name. Ask, and you will receive, that your joy may be full."*. Friendship with God creates the overwhelming, overflowing joy of Christ in you. Burdens are lighter, blessings are better, and valleys more tolerable when you are in friendship with God. Friendship with God overthrows frustration and makes each day not only bearable, but incredible! Through conversations with God you will learn to trust Him. He is a Father who can always be trusted.

Jesus said, "Ask, and it will be given to you; seek, and you will find; knock, and it will be opened to you. For everyone who asks receives, and he who seeks finds, and to him who knocks it will be opened. Or what man is there among you who, if his son asks for bread, will give him a stone? Or if he asks for a fish, will he give him a serpent? If you then, being evil, know how to give good gifts to your children, how much more will your Father who is in heaven give good things to those who ask Him" Matthew 7:7-11. Jesus wants your life to be full of His joy. It's a huge part of the abundant life He promises. It all starts with conversations just like Jesus had with the Father. Jesus paid a very high price for you to enjoy sweet fellowship and communion with Him. Step in and enjoy friendship with God. Your prayer life will never be the same again.

Declaration of Joy: "Heavenly Father, I am so thankful that You pursued friendship with me. It's beyond my comprehension that You've done so, but I am so grateful that You did. I will always remind myself of how You've opened the door of communion with You, and gladly invited me to fellowship with You forever. I will walk with You, and talk with You in all my ways, for all my days. Thank You for answers that have come, and for the ones that will yet be granted, but most of all, thank You for the forever conversation You and I are enjoying right now. It truly is the greatest joy of my life."

CHAPTER 6

"JOY IN TRIALS"

"My brethren, count it all joy when you fall into various trials, knowing that the testing of your faith produces patience. But let patience have its perfect work, that you may be perfect and complete, lacking nothing."
James 1:2-4

Trials are tough. No one likes them. Nevertheless, we all face them and we all must persevere through them. They can cause worry and fear to manifest in our lives. Trials can be devastating too, for the one who is not quite prepared to walk through them. Have you or others you know been through a recent trial? Has losing a loved one, or experiencing disappointment, or a tragedy diminished you emotionally, spiritually, or relationally? Trials can wound you and drain you in so many ways. Your soul can languish under the weight of needless burdens if relief and healing are not soon applied. Are you one who has walked through a difficult trial lately, or perhaps you are in one now? Whatever the case, I have good news for you. It's the joy of the Lord that will sustain you and lift you above the storm.

Counting all things joy when facing a trail is not a natural disposition, it is a supernatural one. No one relishes facing a hardship, or a severe test of faith, but if one is standing in your path right now the Father wants you to know this important truth – He is with you! One of the great reasons you can count all things joy when you face trials of faith is that you know the Father is right there with you and will doubtless bring you out on the other side better and stronger than when you entered it. You may not know when the end will be or know how the Father will do it, but you know He will bring you out on the other side victorious in every way. Therefore, whatever the trial is you can face it with confidence and joy instead of uncertainty, doubts, and fear. As you humble your heart before Him, He will be with you to guide you, empower you, and grow you through pressure. The apostle Peter said, *"The Lord knows how to deliver the godly out of temptations" 2 Peter 2:9* and this power promise includes you!

Fear has no right in your heart and mind when walking with Jesus through a trial of faith. When Satan tries to bring dread and anxiety to your soul, immediately rebuke him and replace his lies with declarations of God's word and deliverance. Willingness to confront the devil with words of faith and victory are important in trial. Complaining only delays your breakthrough. Murmuring hinders the learning process of becoming more like Jesus. On the other hand, faith and trust toward God with patience is the key to spiritual breakthrough, growth, and maturity through trial. You've heard it said, "Patience is a virtue"? Well, faith and patience are virtues you do not want to compromise when walking with the Lord through the valley.

There is no shortage of faith and patience in God's presence. They are easily accessible when you face trials. The Spirit of God is your supplier and He is always present and willing to impart them. It is faith and patience together in trial that will make room in your soul for the joy of the Lord to flourish. Joy springs up in your soul when faith and patience are activated in your trial. Without faith and patience, joy will not manifest as powerfully as you need in your test. Faith, patience, and joy feed each other in trial, building you up in your personal and spiritual life. Through joyful endurance Christ-like maturity is produced in your life for all to see and you to enjoy.

Your joy in trial is an encouragement to others. It helps them face their trials courageously. Your joy in trial is an amazing display of God's power to those on the fence, or those who have never given their life to Christ. When they see you advancing with an unexplainable joy in your heart it truly is a sign and wonder to them. I strongly believe the Holy Spirit is always working to strategically position joy filled Christians among the most cynical and wounded people in our world. Why? Instead of bitterness from a believer in trial, the lost person observes joy, faith, and perseverance. How important is it for those who do know Christ to see Christ working in you this way? This is genuine power from God at work in you. It truly gives people hope that they can have the joy of the Lord in their pain and difficulty as well. It's not just miracles and healings that the lost want to see from you, it's sincerity, transparency, peace, and joy in hardship.

Your trial is an opportunity to demonstrate what a real Christian looks like in unfavorable and difficult situations. It's your time to shine, beloved. When things aren't so perfect, you can be a light to others. People need to see the fruit of joy manifesting in your life, and humble patience maturing you spiritually. When you let joy and patience work in you, the bible says you will fully mature in Christ and be completely equipped for every test of life.

Declaration of Joy: "Heavenly Father, thank You for faith, patience and joy. Thank You for what they produce in me when I endeavor to live by them in the trials I face. Please forgive me for not walking in these amazing virtues of the Spirit of God. Help equip me to prepare my heart and mind with them. I declare by faith, that Your joy, patience, and faith will work perfectly together as I intentionally live by them. I refuse to get caught up in my fleshly actions of impatience, frustration, and anger in trial! I resist the temptation to act impatiently toward anyone in my pain. Rather, I will lift my eyes of faith to You, knowing that as I look to You, I will enjoy greater fellowship with You and shine with Christ's light of joy to those around me. In the great Name of Jesus I pray, Amen!"

CHAPTER 7

"THE JOY SET BEFORE YOU"

"Therefore, we also, since we are surrounded by so great a cloud of witnesses, let us lay aside every weight, and the sin which so easily ensnares us, and let us run with endurance the race that is set before us, looking unto Jesus, the author and finisher of our faith, who for the joy that was set before Him endured the cross, despising the shame, and has sat down at the right hand of the throne of God."
Hebrews 12:1-2

When you plan a vacation, the first thing you do is envision the destination. Before you ever get there, you see yourself enjoying the beach, or the mountains, or a hammock in the shade. Then, comes the planning. Every detail needs to be covered, at least for most of us micromanagers. Saving money and sacrificing other things is usually a part of the planning. Finally, the day arrives for packing. All the necessities, amenities, and clothes are carefully packed and placed so you do not forget a thing. Then comes traveling to the destination. Sometimes this is one of the most enjoyable parts of the vacation. Anticipating the experience and all you sacrificed is on the horizon. Truly, well planned vacations are the best vacations, at least in my mind.

On the other hand, a poorly planned vacation can be disastrous. Instead of a blessing, it can become a burden. That fact is any measure of success you achieve at something worthwhile usually occurs through good planning and a willingness to sacrifice. In a career or an important cause, preparation and sacrifice are a must to achieve your goals. Jesus understood this principle of success. He knew His purpose, planned His path, and completed the plan. He poured out His life as a sacrifice for the world. But what sustained Him through all the rejection and pain of His earthly ministry? Without question it was *"the joy set before Him"*! It was the anticipation of seeing salvation's plan for all mankind accomplished.

Jesus understood the destination for His life was to ultimately pass through the cross of Calvary. I'm not sure at what age He received this difficult revelation from the Father, but it came nonetheless, and He accepted it. He knew He would endure mocking, scourging, false accusations and so much more from the people, the soldiers, and the elders of Israel, but He also knew what the result would be – eternal life for all who believed in Him. From the beginning of His earthly ministry, He saw how He would lay down His life and die to fulfill the Father's redemption plan. In the Garden of Gethsemane, as He faced the darkest moment of His life, it was the vision and joy beyond the cross that sustained Him. *"Let this cup pass from me. Nevertheless, not my will, but yours be done"*, He prayed. Jesus faced the pain and death of crucifixion by seeing the joyful end of a dreadful process. He saw the joy of resurrection and life eternal for all.

By faith, Jesus envisioned the triumphant end of His great journey. The Father showed it to Him, and He was willing to fully embrace it from beginning to end. In much the same way, the Father is showing you the fruitful end of your trial. The question is, are you seeing what the Father is revealing to you? Do you see the triumphant end of your trial, your life's work, your ministry, study, and sacrifice? Jesus does! Do you see the good things your trial is producing in you, through you, and for those you know and serve? Are you willing to face sacrifice and struggle to reach your destination of blessings? If you can see it, and sense the joy of the Father in it, you can carry your cross through to the end. For the joy that was set before Him on the other side of the cross, Jesus endured the shame and triumphed over it all.

Do you know every trial the Father allows you to go through has a purpose? Not only is the Father maturing you and bringing hope to others through your witness, but He is also going to raise you up to share with them the victory Christ gives. Trials are never meant to crush you. Trials are meant to mature you and promote you. The world needs those who sit with Christ, at rest with Him through adversity in this life. People need to see how you learned to walk through the fire and not be burned. They need to learn the secret of seeing the joy set before and the victory on the other side. Do you see your trials this way? If you see the joy ahead, you will never view your trials of faith and sacrifice for Christ the same again!

Make no mistake about it, the devil will come to steal your joy and blind you with pain to keep you from seeing to the crown of victory on the other side. It's easy to lose sight of what's set before you when you're hit with Satan's lies and deceptions. Your victory over him in your struggle depends not only on your faith to overcome, but your joy to persevere as well. Together they uplift you in the battle. If faith is the victory that overcomes the world, joy is the laughter along the way! The devil knows if he can kill your joy, he can delay your victory. When you see beyond your trial to what it will produce for your Heavenly Father, you gladly rise in faith and joy, like Jesus did to meet your challenge. Above the storms of life, you soar, to the blue skies of exaltation and revelation with Christ. Your trials have no power over you when you endure them with the faith Christ gives you and His joy that empowers you.

The Hebrew writer encourages us to run the race set before us with patience, looking unto Jesus, the author and finisher of our faith. It was Jesus who led the way blazing the trail of faith with the joy. He pleased the Father in all things, seeing the eternal results of His glad obedience. The joy that was set before Jesus sustained Him and helped Him endure the cross and the shame. Now, He is seated at the right hand of the Father, intimately involved with you, helping you overcome with joy all the way to the finish line.

Declaration of Joy: "Heavenly Father, thank You for helping me see beyond the trials I'm facing into the great fruit it will produce. Thank You that You always have my victory planned before I ever see it myself. My confidence is in You! Help me to yield to Your precious Holy Spirit so I can be filled with Your joy through my trials. Give me prophetic vision to see beyond the pain all the way to blessing. Let Your joy in me be a mighty witness to others. Let them see that You are just as real in trials as you are in triumphs. Let Your light of joy shine through me in every peak and valley I walk through. Let Your joy empower my faith. Let my faith in You be my continual victory that overcomes the world. In the name of Jesus I pray, Amen!"

CHAPTER 8

"THE MANIFEST PRESENCE OF GOD"

"You will show me the path of life; In Your presence is fullness of joy; At Your right hand are pleasures forevermore."
Psalms 16:11

God is omnipresent. He is always everywhere each moment. His Holy Spirit makes this possible. Just like the air we breathe is everywhere, and the wind that blows across the face of the earth is everywhere, so God's presence is everywhere interacting with all living things on the planet. Since God is omnipresent, He is always with you and benevolently mindful of you. What an amazing thought! The omnipresence of God defies human logic and comprehension, yet to the one who believes, it is wonderfully comprehensible, altogether simple, pure, and sweet to the soul.

The psalmist wrote, *"O LORD, You have searched me and known me. You know my sitting down and my rising up; You understand my thoughts afar off. You comprehend my path and my lying down and are acquainted with all my ways. For there is not a word on my tongue, but behold, O LORD, You know it altogether. You have hedged me behind and before and laid Your hand upon me. Such knowledge is too wonderful for me; It is high, I cannot attain it. Where can I go from Your Spirit? Or where can I flee from Your presence? If I ascend into* heaven, You are there; If I make my bed in hell, behold, You are there. If I take the wings of the morning, and dwell in the uttermost parts of the sea, even there Your hand shall lead me, and Your right hand shall hold me" Psalms 139:1-10.

Awareness of the Father's presence is just the beginning of communion with Him. Intimacy and friendship are what the Father is seeking most from you. They are the greatest treasures a soul can experience. Right now, Jesus invites you to abide with Him in the presence of the Father. Jesus said, *"Come to Me, all you who labor and are heavy laden, and I will give you rest. Take My yoke upon you and learn from Me, for I am gentle and lowly in heart, and you will find rest for your souls. For My yoke is easy and My burden is light"* Matthew 11:28-29. He invites you, not just to know about the omnipresence of God, but to experience the manifest presence of God – and there is a theological and doctrinal difference between the two. The omnipresence of God is about the awareness of God in the world. The manifest presence is about personal and transformational intimacy with God in the heart. Knowing about His omnipresence is wonderful indeed, but experiencing His love, closeness, and communion in your life is what the manifest presence of God is all about.

The word "manifest" means to make clear and obvious to the eye, mind, and senses. As a verb, the word manifest means the act of displaying, showing, or demonstrating the quality or feeling of something, in this case the very presence of Almighty God. Jesus said this about the manifest presence of God. *"He who has My commandments and keeps them, it is he who loves Me. And he who loves Me* will be loved by My Father, and I will love him and manifest Myself to him" John 14:21*. Jesus explains in this verse that the manifest presence of God is experienced through love and devotion to the Son and His commandments. He says the Father responds to those who love the Son this way by manifesting His glory presence in their life.

When you gave your life to Jesus Christ, you were immediately ushered into the Father's manifest presence. The apostle Paul wrote, *"You are the temple of the living God. As God has said: 'I will dwell in them and walk among them. I will be their God, and they shall be My people. Therefore, come out from among them and be separate, says the Lord. Do not touch what is unclean, and I will receive you. I will be a Father to you, and you shall be My sons and daughters, says the LORD Almighty'" II Corinthians 6:16-18*. Right now, the Father is making Himself known to you. When your response to His Son is love and devotion, He promises to manifest His presence in your life. When your vision is Jesus, the Father's pleasure and joy will be yours. When you learn to love the Son with the Father's love for Him, you will continually abide with them in their tangible love.

Do you want the joy and pleasure that the psalmist spoke about? Ask the Holy Spirit to ignite your heart with the Father's love for His Son! Your heart will feast on the fullness of joy found there. Your soul will rest in the pleasure of knowing Jesus and abiding in the Father's love. The path of life that leads to the manifest presence of the Father is love for His Son. Therefore, with confidence declare to the Father, "You have shown me the path of life, and it is Jesus Christ! In Your presence is the fullness of joy, and that joy is in Your Son! At Your right hand are pleasures forevermore, and those forever pleasures are in Jesus, my Savior and King!"

Declaration of Joy: "Heavenly Father, I gladly receive Your Son, Jesus Christ into my heart afresh and anew! I believe with all my heart that He died on the cross for my sin and rose from the dead for my justification. Thank You Lord Jesus, for the power of Your blood that cleanses me from all my sin, guilt, and shame. Come into my heart, Lord Jesus! Fill me with Your Holy Spirit. Empower me to live for You so I can learn to abide in Your manifest presence continually. I thank You for the joy that awaits me every day as I seek You and walk with You. Your manifest presence is my resting place. Your presence of limitless joy and pleasures are my great treasures in this life. Thank You for it all! In the mighty name of Jesus I pray. Amen!"

CHAPTER 9

"THE JOY OF BROKENNESS"

"Those who sow in tears shall reap in joy. He who continually goes forth weeping, bearing seed for sowing, shall doubtless come again with rejoicing, bringing his sheaves with him."
Psalms 126:5-6

In Christ, brokenness is a blessing, humility brings promotion, and meekness and lowliness are rewarded. Tears are honored in the kingdom of God. They are not despised. Tears are not a sign of weakness, but rather a sign of strength, conviction, and compassion. Weeping is remembered by God. Tears are stored in His bottle of hope and written about in His books. When you cry to God, your enemies face defeat. The psalmist writes, *"Put my tears into Your bottle; Are they not in Your book? When I cry out to You, then my enemies will turn back; This I know, because God is for me"* Psalm 56:8-9. Again the psalmist says, *"For You do not desire sacrifice, or else I would give it; You do not delight in burnt offering. The sacrifices of God are a broken spirit, a broken and a contrite heart— These, O God, You will not despise"* Psalms 51:16-17.

Tears are what we sow in the presence of God when we are asking heartfelt things of Him. For souls to be saved, people to be healed, and loved ones to be delivered, weeping is the measure of triumph. Brokenness of soul is a powerfully meaningful message to God. Tears demonstrate your anguish and compassion before the God of all compassion. Groanings from your spirit are desired in the throne room of your Heavenly Father. His Son poured out His soul in anguish as an offering for the sin of others, and at times you must do the same for others. Isaiah wrote, *"Yet it pleased the Lord to bruise Him; He has put Him to grief. When You make His soul an offering for sin, He shall see His seed, He shall prolong His days, and the pleasure of the Lord shall prosper in His hand"* Isaiah 53:10. Our Great Intercessor, Jesus Christ was heard by God, and by man weeping in the days of His flesh. The word tells us, *"Who, in the days of His flesh, when He had offered up prayers and supplications, with vehement cries and tears to Him who was able to save Him from death, and was heard because of His godly fear, though He was a Son, yet He learned obedience by the things which He suffered. And having been perfected, He became the author of eternal salvation to all who obey Him"* Hebrews 5:7-9.

Tears are a language that your Heavenly Father and your Savior know very well. That's why the psalmist writes, *"Those who sow in tears shall reap in joy."* Tears are powerful seeds that come from the heart of the children of light. Into the darkness of a sinful world they fall, bright with the hope of the gospel's power to save, heal, and fill people with the Holy Spirit. When tears flow from the heart of a child of God, sons and daughters of God are born again. Nothing from hell can stop the blessing that brokenness brings forth in the sight of God.

When you are armed with tears, demons tremble. As lambs among wolves the child of God goes forth bearing the gospel and sowing it with tears. Your tears are not a sign of regret, they are a sign of surrender. Surrender to the will of the Father to seek and save the lost. With tears you are sent to those who have never heard the good news, and to those who have never experienced the God of love. You plant the seed of the gospel with your tears, and water it with the same. It's in this process of brokenness and planting that the Father whispers, "It's only a matter of time and the answer will come." The Father plans it this way. Tears and brokenness precede and expedite the harvest.

Paul the Apostle wrote, *"I planted, Apollos watered, but God gave the increase. So then neither he who plants is anything, nor he who waters, but God who gives the increase. Now he who plants and he who waters are one, and each one will receive his own reward according to his own labor"* I Corinthians 3:6-8. A harvest of souls awaits those who sow the gospel with tears. Many are swept into the kingdom of God through rivers of tears. When the child of God embraces brokenness for the lost, the lost will be saved. "Those who sow in tears shall reap in joy. He who continually goes forth weeping, bearing seed for sowing, shall doubtless come again with rejoicing, bringing his sheaves with him." Let the truth of these words burn in you like a fire!

If you are burdened about the eternal destiny of a loved one or friend, you need not feel helpless to see them saved. Do you have tears? Then you have power with God, and seed to sow! Sow your tears in the eternal soil of God's love for the lost! Sow them today! Sow them tomorrow and the next day, and the next. Go with tears to your prayer closet and go forth with the gospel in your heart. You will doubtless return with joy, bringing your sheaves with you – precious souls, whom you love won to Christ.

Declaration of Joy: "Heavenly Father, I pray the words of the Prophet, Jeremiah *'Oh, that my head were waters, and my eyes a fountain of tears, that I might weep day and night for the slain of the daughter of my people' Jeremiah 9:1.* Let my hardness be turned to weeping for the lost in my family, among my friends and neighbors. Awaken Your burden in me for those who are helpless and hopeless against Satan's bondage. Break my heart for those who are sick and afflicted without soundness and wholeness in their body. Jesus, You are the Savior! You are the Healer! Let Your compassion move me like it moved You. Let tears be my glad portion until souls come home to You, and to the House of God. Let the harvest you've determined come forth with weeping and with gladness, and I will give You all the praise! In the precious Name of Jesus I pray, Amen!"

CHAPTER 10

"THE JOY OF SALVATION & THE SUPERNATURAL"

"Then the seventy returned with joy, saying, 'Lord, even the demons are subject to us in Your name.' And He said to them, 'I saw Satan fall like lightning from Heaven. Behold, I give you the authority to trample on serpents and scorpions, and over all the power of the enemy, and nothing shall by any means hurt you. Nevertheless, do not rejoice in this, that the spirits are subject to you, but rather rejoice because your names are written in Heaven."
Luke 10:17-20

Jesus said He saw Satan fall from Heaven. This implies Satan had his abode in Heaven before he sinned and was cast out. The Prophet Isaiah wrote, *"How you are fallen from heaven, O Lucifer, son of the morning! How you are cut down to the ground, you who weakened the nations! For you have said in your heart: 'I will ascend into heaven, I will exalt my throne above the stars of God; I will also sit on the mount of the congregation on the farthest sides of the north; I will ascend above the heights of the clouds, I will be like the Most High.' Yet you shall be brought down to Sheol, to the lowest depths of the pit"* Isaiah 14:12-15. Lucifer, another name for Satan, had his abode in Heaven, and was known as a beautiful cherub who worshipped God in Heaven. The prophet goes on to describe Satan after his fall, *"Those who see you will gaze at you, and consider you, saying: 'Is this the one who made the earth tremble, who shook kingdoms, who made the world as a wilderness and destroyed its cities, who did not open the house of his prisoners?'" (Isaiah 14:15-17).*

Ezekiel adds even more, *"You were in Eden, the garden of God; Every precious stone was your covering: The sardius, topaz, and diamond, beryl, onyx, and jasper, sapphire, turquoise, and emerald with gold. The workmanship of your timbrels and pipes was prepared for you on the day you were created. You were the anointed cherub who covers; I established you; You were on the holy mountain of God; You walked back and forth in the midst of fiery stones. You were perfect in your ways from the day you were created, till iniquity was found in you. You became filled with violence within, and you sinned; Therefore I cast you as a profane thing out of the mountain of God; And I destroyed you, O covering cherub, from the midst of the fiery stones. Your heart was lifted up because of your beauty; You corrupted your wisdom for the sake of your splendor; I cast you to the ground, I laid you before kings, that they might gaze at you. You defiled your sanctuaries by the multitude of your iniquities, by the iniquity of your trading; Therefore I brought fire from your midst; It devoured you, and I turned you to ashes upon the earth in the sight of all who saw you. All who knew you among the peoples are astonished at you; You have become a horror and shall be no more forever." Ezekiel 28:13-19.*

Through pride, Satan ruined his glorious and powerful position as a cherub in Heaven. Jesus describes Satan's instantaneous fall from Heaven as a flash of lightening.

Suddenly, Lucifer was stripped of his glory. The beautifully created cherub was banished to hell and to the dust of the earth. Jesus reminded His followers of this amazing event before He sent them out to preach the gospel and heal the sick. Jesus assured them wherever they were sent, Satan had no power to harm them. He was cast down and they were now given all power and authority over him to free others from demonic influence. They were to go forth preaching the gospel everywhere, and as they went, they were to cast out Satan and his demons just like the Father cast him out of Heaven. This is a very important truth for you to know as a child of God. Satan is cast down, he is defeated and spoiled on every level! He has no power over you, your family, or those to whom you minister. Just like the early disciples did when they went forth to share testimony of Jesus Christ, you too have all power and authority given to you by Jesus to cast out demons and set captives free.

The Bible says, *"Be sober, be vigilant; because your adversary the devil walks about like a roaring lion, seeking whom he may devour. Resist him, steadfast in the faith..."* I Peter 5:8-9. Satan is a ruthless predator. He is seeking to destroy precious souls for whom Jesus died to save. He is your adversary and the adversary of every person born into this world. The apostle Peter encourages us to be very much aware of the devil's evil desire and to resist him continuously in the faith. As a child of God, you have been given the faith of God to not only resist the devil, but to cause him to flee when you confront him. Through the power of the Holy Spirit, the Name of Jesus, the word of God, and the decree of Jesus, you now have dominion over

Satan and the kingdom of darkness. Satan is very much aware of this declaration and impartation, and as the *"father of lies"*, he will do everything in his power to keep you from walking in it. Like a cruel manipulator and murderer, Satan deceives and connives to kill, steal, and destroy. The Bible says, *"Inasmuch then as the children have partaken of flesh and blood, He Himself likewise shared in the same, that through death He might destroy him who had the power of death, that is, the devil, and release those who through fear of death were all their lifetime subject to bondage"* Hebrews 2:14-15. The Apostle John wrote, *"For this purpose the Son of God was manifested, that He might destroy the works of the devil"* I John 3:8. This is your purpose too. You are to destroy the destroyer and his influence by the authority and power that Jesus gives you.

In His earthly ministry Jesus demonstrated the authority He had over Satan through many signs, wonders and miracles. The disciples watched in amazement as Jesus crushed Satan's influence and kingdom wherever He went. As the son of man, Jesus turned the tide of Satan's power against mankind with every word and work of His hand. When Jesus gave the disciples His power and authority to cast out demons, heal the sick and preach the gospel everything changed for Adam's fallen race. Satan's defeat was imminent. When Jesus sent them out two by two, He told them not to fear anything because they had the same authority and power in their words, actions, and prayers as He did. Not even snakes or scorpions could harm them. They were ordained by Christ and empowered by Him. As a child of God, you too are deputized to carry out Christ's supernatural ministry of healing the sick, casting out demons, and teaching the good news. You are authorized by Him to bring the kingdom of God to everyone around you. You possess the same Holy Spirit Jesus possessed in order to face the same challenges He faced, and devastate the one attempting to destroy the ones you love.

Nothing causes joy in the heart of Christian's like seeing others saved, healed, and set free. I am sure when you've prayed for someone and God answered, the first thing to fill your heart was the joy of the Lord for what He had done on your behalf. The Bible says angels rejoice in Heaven over one sinner that repents and turns to God. When those disciples were sent out with the authority of Christ, little did they know the impact they would have on others. Demons immediately came out of people when they spoke. Lepers were instantly healed when they prayed. The dead were raised to life again and the joy of the Lord was renewed in the hearts of the people wherever they went. They were amazed at it all and so were the people. Day after day miraculous things happened as they traveled from village to village. Their joy level was soaring. Revival and awakening were happening all at once. Surely, the kingdom of God was here, and it was glorious!

When seventy returned to report all the amazing things that were done, Jesus had a word for them, a reminder that they would not forget. It was simple and to the point, and a great reminder for them and for all Christ's followers throughout the ages. *"Nevertheless, do not rejoice in this, that the spirits are subject to you, but rather rejoice because your names are written in Heaven."* He was not rebuking them for rejoicing about all the good that was done through them, He was prompting them to remember, above all else, the greatest of all things the Father had done for them; Their names were written in Heaven! The authority they had over Satan and his influence in the world was good, but the joy of their salvation was greater. Without question, Jesus wants all His disciples to move in His power to heal and deliver the oppressed, but most of all He wants them to rejoice in the Father and His great saving grace. The prophet Isaiah said, *"Behold, God is my salvation, I will trust and not be afraid; 'For YAH, the LORD, is my strength and song; He also has become my salvation. Therefore, with joy you will draw water from the wells of salvation. And in that day you will say: 'Praise the LORD, call upon His name; Declare His deeds among the peoples, make mention that His name is exalted. Sing to the LORD, for He has done excellent things; This is known in all the earth" Isaiah 12:2-5.*

Your authority and power over Satan are very important to God. Good things come to the hurting because believers like you who are empowered by the Spirit of God obey the Great Commission of Christ and set captive sinners free. Make no mistake about it, the Father loves to crush Satan's bondage through you. However, nothing is of greater importance, and nothing is a greater source of joy in your life than the joy of knowing your name is written in the Lambs Book of Life. The Bible says, *"I saw no temple in it, for the Lord God Almighty and the Lamb are its temple. The city had no need of the sun or of the moon to shine in it, for the glory of God illuminated it. The Lamb is its light. And the nations of those who are saved shall walk in its light, and the kings of the earth bring their glory and honor into it. Its gates shall not be shut at all by day (there shall be no night there).*

And they shall bring the glory and the honor of the nations into it. But there shall by no means enter it anything that defiles, or causes an abomination or a lie, but only those who are written in the Lamb's Book of Life." Revelation 21:22-27

I have found in my forty years of serving Christ, when my source of joy in life is Jesus, I never lack for the miraculous power of God in my life. Jesus always supplies His yoke breaking anointing to the one who holds true to their first love for Him. Darkness will always flee before those who walk in the light with Jesus. The fact is Satan is no match for the Saint who lives in the perfect balance of God's power and the joy of their salvation! The words Jesus spoke are still as potent today as they were when His disciples returned rejoicing. Read them again and let them teach you perfect spiritual balance between the supernatural gifts of the Holy Spirit and the joy of your first love. *"Behold, I give you the authority to trample on serpents and scorpions, and over all the power of the enemy, and nothing shall by any means hurt you. Nevertheless, do not rejoice in this, that the spirits are subject to you, but rather rejoice because your names are written in Heaven." Luke 10:19-20.* You are a powerful witness for God when you walk in the light of these truths. You will bring great hope and joy to others when you live to demonstrate peace with God and the power of God." Amen!

Declaration of Joy: "Heavenly Father, thank You for the miraculous things You do in me and through me. I embrace them and prepare my heart for even more works of Your power. Most of all, I thank You for my salvation. Thank You that my name is written in Heaven and my life is filled with the joy of eternal life in Christ. I pray Your mighty acts and miraculous works will continue to accompany all that I do for you, but above all else I pray the joy of my first love and fellowship with You will grow like never before. In the wonderful Name of Jesus I pray, Amen!"

CHAPTER 11

"THE JOY OF THE WHOLE EARTH"

"Beautiful in elevation, the joy of the whole earth, is Mount Zion on the sides of the north, the city of the great King."
Psalms 48:2

Mount Zion is three things according to this verse. First, it is beautiful. Second, it is the joy of the whole earth. Third, it is the city of the great King! For ancient Israel, Mount Zion was the mountain where the city of Jerusalem was built. The word "Zion" appears 152 times in the Old Testament as the name of Jerusalem. Most of those references to Zion are found in two books, the Book of Isaiah 46 times, and the Book of Psalms 38 times. It is referenced only seven times in the New Testament. The deeply emotional, spiritual, and prophetic qualities of Mount Zion emerge from the importance of Jerusalem as the place of the presence of Yahweh, the God of Israel, and where He is worshipped. The Bible tells us that Mount Zion, the Mountain of God is the place where the King of Kings, the Messiah, Jesus will set up His earthly Kingdom in all its splendor and will be worshiped by all kings and nations of the earth.

In the Book of Revelation, we read amazing things about our glorious King Jesus, the future of His beautiful city of Zion and His Kingdom reign on the earth. *"But I saw no* temple in it, for the Lord God Almighty and the Lamb are its temple. The city had no need of the sun or of the moon to shine in it, for the glory of God illuminated it. The Lamb is its light. And the nations of those who are saved shall walk in its light, and the kings of the earth bring their glory and honor into it. Its gates shall not be shut at all by day (there shall be no night there). And they shall bring the glory and the honor of the nations into it. But there shall by no means enter it anything that defiles, or causes an abomination or a lie, but only those who are written in the Lamb's Book of Life" Revelation 21:22-27. This is the fulfillment of Psalm 48:2, "Beautiful in elevation, the joy of the whole earth, is Mount Zion on the sides of the north, the city of the great King."

In the book of Hebrews, we read about Mount Zion and its ever-increasing glory and power in the earth. *"For you have not come to the mountain that may be touched and that burned with fire, and to blackness and darkness and tempest, and the sound of a trumpet and the voice of words, so that those who heard it begged that the word should not be spoken to them anymore. (For they could not endure what was commanded: 'And if so much as a beast touches the mountain, it shall be stoned or shot with an arrow.' And so terrifying was the sight that Moses said, 'I am exceedingly afraid and trembling.) But you have come to Mount Zion and to the City of the Living God, the Heavenly Jerusalem, to an innumerable company of angels, to the General Assembly and Church of the Firstborn who are registered in Heaven, to God the Judge of all, to the spirits of just men made perfect, to Jesus the Mediator of the New Covenant, and to the blood of sprinkling that speaks better things than that of Abel. See that you do not refuse Him who speaks. For if they did not escape who *refused Him who spoke on earth, much more shall we not escape if we turn away from Him who speaks from Heaven, whose Voice then shook the earth; but now He has promised, saying, 'Yet once more I shake not only the earth, but also Heaven.' Now this, 'Yet once more,' indicates the removal of those things that are being shaken, as of things that are made, that the things which cannot be shaken may remain. Therefore, since we are receiving a kingdom which cannot be shaken, let us have grace, by which we may serve God acceptably with reverence and godly fear. For our God is a consuming fire" Hebrews 12:18-29.* What do you think of this magnificent sight? Could it be any more beautiful? Could it be any more powerful? Do you see the glory and grandeur of Mount Zion, the city of the great King? Do you feel the trembling and reverence that emanate from it? Can you comprehend the brilliance of it all? It is beautiful in its elevation and vastness. This is Mount Zion, the unmovable, unshakable, undeniable, unstoppable Mountain of God that exists eternally and is manifesting through followers of Jesus in the earth. It grows in scope, power, and grace through believers winning souls, casting out demons, healing the sick, discipling nations, building churches, preaching the gospel, and advancing the kingdom of the great King.

Do you see Zion as the delight of the whole earth? Do others see it too? Jesus said they can if they are born of the Spirit. In John chapter three we read, *"Most assuredly, I say to you, unless one is born again, he cannot see the kingdom of God. Nicodemus said to Him, 'How can a man be born when he is old? Can he enter a second time into his mother's womb and be born?' Jesus answered, 'Most assuredly, I say to you, unless one is born of water and the Spirit, he cannot enter the kingdom of God.'"* Since you have been born of the Spirit through faith in Jesus Christ, you can not only see the kingdom of God, you have already entered it. Prophetic vision to see the kingdom is your spiritual birthright. All who are born of the Spirit have spiritual eyes to see God's vast, beautiful, and eternal kingdom. As sons and daughters of God you are able to perceive its expansion with every new soul saved and life transformed. You see as it shakes every kingdom of men and causes the kingdom of darkness to flee. You are a vital participant in the greatest building project in human history, the Church of the first born, the building of God. The kingdom of the great King is shaking and removing all other kingdoms that resists Heaven's rule! This is our Father's world and He will have His way.

Jesus gave us a powerful glimpse into how His kingdom is growing and Mount Zion is increasing in the earth when He said, *"The kingdom of God does not come with observation; nor will they say, 'See here!' or 'See there!' For indeed, the kingdom of God is within you"* Luke 17:20-21. What does this mean? It means since the King and His kingdom dwells in you, you are already as much a part of the Eternal City as you are of your earthly habitation. You are both seated with Christ reigning and ruling with Him as well as carrying out God's kingdom authority against hostile enemies in our world. Without question God's kingdom advance is an imminent threat to all who oppose and reject it, but it is joy and a cause for rejoicing to all those who believe and receive it. It causes great delight in the heart of the humble, but great dread in the heart of the haughty.

The Psalmist gives us a glimpse into the resistance of the haughty and the powerful toward the King and the kingdom of Heaven. *"Why do the nations rage, and the people plot a vain thing? The kings of the earth set themselves, and the rulers take counsel together, against the Lord and against His Anointed, saying, 'Let us break Their bonds in pieces and cast away Their cords from us.' He who sits in the Heavens shall laugh; The Lord shall hold them in derision. Then He shall speak to them in His wrath, and distress them in His deep displeasure: 'Yet I have set My King on My holy hill of Zion. I will declare the decree: The Lord has said to Me, 'You are My Son, today I have begotten You. Ask of Me, and I will give You the nations for Your inheritance, and the ends of the earth for Your possession. You shall break them with a rod of iron; You shall dash them to pieces like a potter's vessel.' Now therefore, be wise, O kings; Be instructed, you Judges of the earth. Serve the Lord with fear and rejoice with trembling. Kiss the Son, lest He be angry, and you perish in the way, when His wrath is kindled but a little. Blessed are all those who put their trust in Him"* - Psalm 2.   Mount Zion is beautiful, it's King is beautiful, the result of its expansion in the earth is beautiful. "Kiss the Son", the Psalmist says. This phrase implies your affection and love for Jesus give you access to the unshakable and unstoppable kingdom that is Mount Zion. It is the joy of the whole earth. It is glorious in every way. It is your city! It is your eternal home! It is the city of your great and glorious King."

Declaration of Joy: "Heavenly Father, thank You for Your kingdom and for your desire to welcome me into it. I enter its gates with thanksgiving. I enter its courts with praise! Thank You for Your Son, the Light of the world, the

Light of Your great City! Thank You for prophetic vision to see it, to understand it, and to enjoy it. Thank You for its sure foundation in my life and future. Thank You that your kingdom dwells within me, and I dwell within Your kingdom. I will forever see myself as a citizen of the City of the Great King. I will walk in His light, His power, and His love. I will help others find it, enter it, and enjoy it. Your kingdom and influence are always expanding, and I want to be a part of that growth. I will always seek to be a builder of Your Church and advance Your glorious Kingdom. In the great Name of Jesus I pray, amen!"

CHAPTER 12

"THE JOY OF JESUS"

"But now I come to You, and these things I speak in the world, that they may have My joy fulfilled in themselves."
John 17:13

In John 17, you are invited to sit and listen to an intimate conversation between the Father and the Son. As you listen, you can sense the beating heart of Jesus as He speaks to the Father about His imminent passion. The bible says He, *"lifted up His eyes to Heaven and said, Father, the hour has come..."*. His emotion was real as He looked up and spoke to the Father. Attentively the Father listened as the Son poured out His heart. In this moment we see the Father and Son face to face, heart to heart, flame to flame for the purpose of redemption. This is a glimpse into the eternal relationship of the Godhead. It is a conversation like none that had ever existed between the sons of man and the God of man, an exchange that would change the world forever.

Jesus was only hours away from a cruel death, yet He remained steadfast and determined to honor the Father and bring salvation to the world. In this passage, Jesus invites us to see and hear perfect oneness and openness with the Father. Even His body language declared assurance in the Father as He *"lifted up His eyes to Heaven"*. Among so many wonderful things Jesus prayed in this dreadful moment, there is one request He breathed out that I do not want you to miss. He said, *"I now come to You, and these things I speak in the world, that they may have My joy fulfilled in themselves."* Can there be any greater request for His disciples than for His disciples to experience His eternal joy fulfilled in them? Joy that can never be diminished, changed, taken away, shaken, or destroyed. In this moment Jesus does not ask the Father to fill His disciples with supernatural power from the Spirit, nor does He request that they be given supernatural revelation or gifts from the Father for ministry. Rather, He simply asks the Father to give them His perfect joy. Jesus knew His disciples would need it in the coming years of ministry for Him. He knew the terrible persecution they would face as they went forth everywhere preaching the gospel. It would be His joy that would sustain them through it all, just like it sustained Him through mocking and crucifixion.

The joy of Jesus has divine strength unlike anything else He could give you. It empowers you to overcome the things opposing your witness in the world. Joy emboldens the Christ-follower in the most difficult circumstances. It lightens life's burden and lifts the spirit to soar. No matter what the struggle, the joy of Lord will fill you with hope in every time. Jesus prayed for you to fully experience His joy in every spiritual battle and disappointment. It is what you need to walk through emotional valleys and pressures of life. You may not fully understand how the joy of the Lord works in hard times, but rest assured, the Spirit of Jesus knows how to deliver it to you in your hours of great testing, and it is a mighty witness to those around you

When you determine to live in the joy of Jesus not everyone will understand you. I've discovered over decades of living in His joy that it confounds the unbeliever and the cynic. When you walk through fiery trials with the joy of Jesus radiating through your life, some will think it's fake, or a religious facade. To them the joy of the Lord seems unrealistic when your faith and trust in God is severely tested. The fact is, you will always have critics, but do not be concerned with them. Their bewilderment just might turn to hope someday when they face real hardship. The joy of the Lord in a believer's life is a great witness to the unbeliever and detractor. Even the lukewarm and the backslidden will be reminded of what they can possess once more if they return to full devotion in Christ. His joy fulfilled in you is a beaming light to those in darkness, and a spark of hope to a perishing world. His joy makes you shine in your darkest hours and emerge vindicated from your weakest seasons in life. His joy fulfilled in you will help others see that the Father's comfort can be theirs too in their most challenging times.

Beloved, are you lacking joy in your life? Have you been wandering in a spiritual wilderness? Are you emotionally empty and feeling spiritually dry? Do not despair or think that full joy in Jesus will never be yours. You only need to turn your face and your heart upward to the Father, just like Jesus did in the Garden. This is the posture all sons and daughters of light take with the Father of lights. It's how Jesus conversed with the Father, and why the Father's joy continually remained in Him. Each day, as you rise from your prayer closet, remember you do not leave your Father's presence, nor does His presence leave you. His fulfilled joy in you need not ever be fragmented by schedules or earthly demands. It is fully given by the Father and will never cease to be yours. Fulfilled joy is always being pour out and can never be quenched. It is completely yours direct from your Heavenly Father.

Beloved, the prayer Jesus prayed that night before He suffered is answered! All you need to do is look up and with faith and confidence receive it. It is unstoppable! It is inexhaustible! It overwhelms all opposition and crushes all lies. Jesus humbly asked the Father, and the Father gladly answered the Son. His joy is what makes life abundant and full, no matter what the adversity. Jesus said, *"The thief does not come except to steal, and to kill, and to destroy. I have come that they may have life, and that they may have it more abundantly. I am the Good Shepherd. The Good Shepherd gives His life for the sheep" John 10:10-11.*

The abundant life Jesus gives includes abundant joy. Some people can have all the money in the world and still not have an abundant life. What makes an abundant life? It's not the things of the world which tarnish and vanish away. It's knowing the Father and the wonderful things He freely gives to His children. Without joy, life would feel empty and dark. I've found that the joy of the Lord turns every negative situation into an oasis of God's presence, blessing, and promotion. Joy gives me access to the treasury of Heaven. On the other hand, murmuring and complaining shut the doors of Heaven. Anger and animosity get me nowhere with God and His provision, but joy supplies His bounty in every trial. So many people wander needlessly in an emotional wilderness because they lack the joy of the

Lord in their life. Look up, my friend, the Father is listening. He is right there and His joy is flowing like a river to you.

One more thing of note before I close this chapter on the joy of Jesus. If you are running low on joy, then you are more than likely running low on patience, kindness, and love too. The joy of the Lord strengthens those virtues in your life. It's the Father's desire to give you the endless joy of Jesus fully, abundantly, and gloriously. He knows the fire of your first love burns brighter on the oil of joy in your heart. He knows your emptiness will vanish away, and your soul will overflow with laughter again when the joy of His Son is abundantly supplied. If I've learned anything over these many years in the Lord's ministry, it's been that my light always shines brighter when my heart is filled with the joy of the Lord. I always feel stronger and more able to overcome when I, by faith look up and receive His abundant supply of joy for me.

Declaration of Joy: "Heavenly Father, thank You for the joy of Jesus and for the glory of His joy fulfilled in me. I will not wander any longer in my wilderness of inward emptiness. I look up and ask You to fulfill in me what Jesus paid such a high price to give me – His overflowing, overpowering, everlasting joy. I will not delay in pursing it, because it's Your heart to give it. Fill me with Your great joy, Lord! Wash away all my despair and hopeless, self-loathing and self-righteousness. I humble myself and look up, to see Your shining face looking back at me. No more gloom and doom for me! Only joy unspeakable and full of glory. Thank You for giving it so freely. Help me to always walk in it and never quench it. I ask this in Jesus' mighty name, Amen!"

CHAPTER 13

"THE REVELATION OF JOY"

> "And Nehemiah, who was the governor, Ezra the priest and scribe, and the Levites who taught the people said to all the people, 'This day is holy to the LORD your God; do not mourn nor weep.' For all the people wept when they heard the words of the Law. Then he said to them, 'Go your way, eat the fat, drink the sweet, and send portions to those for whom nothing is prepared; for this day is holy to our Lord. Do not sorrow, for the joy of the LORD is your strength.' So the Levites quieted all the people, saying, 'Be still, for the day is holy; do not be grieved.' And all the people went their way to eat and drink, to send portions and rejoice greatly, because they understood the words that were declared to them."
> Nehemiah 8:9-12

The revelation of joy is simple, it is a revelation of intimacy, acceptance, and communion with God. The revelation of joy is not based in religious duty or obligation for God. It is a revelation of peace with Him, not pious ritual for Him. Most people do not understand the revelation of the joy of the Lord. They do not understand it because the joy of the Lord is not "performance based". Even though your devotion and service matter greatly to God, those things can never fully produce the joy of the

Lord in your life. Until you realize that you are altogether accepted by the Father as His son or daughter, your service and obligation to Him will always feel somewhat barren and unfulfilling. The joy of knowing you are completely loved by your Heavenly Father and free from religious expectations and duties, is life changing.

Man's religious expectations and laws always seem to give us the wrong impression of God. We know the law of Moses is good, but when it was read to the Jewish people that day, it seemed unattainable to them. They felt they could not meet the religious demands of the Law. It seemed the Law condemned them and made them feel unacceptable to God. The Law of the Lord without a revelation of the joy of the Lord was disheartening to the people of God. They did not understand that it was not about how much they could do for God, but rather how much they were loved by God. Make no mistake about it, this revelation will be tested, and the devil knows how to discourage and test you too. If he can steal your joy, he knows he can zap your strength to resist him as well as zap your strength to achieve great things for God. If he can keep you dejected, he can deter you from accomplishing important things for God. This is a vital point to know when it comes to your service and devotion to God.

Every child of God receives important assignments from their Heavenly Father. Building His church, expanding His kingdom, and setting captives free are all very important works the people of God are to do for Him today. These things take spiritual strength and stamina to achieve. It is the joy of the Lord that supplies much of the spiritual strength you need to accomplish His work. In every way and in every situation, the Lord's joy empowers you for His service. You need not squander any of Heaven's assignments, great or small for lack of strength or resilience. If you have the joy of the Lord in your life, growing weary in the work of the Lord is less likely to manifest in your life. If you want to run the race set before you and keep your heart brimming with the joy of the Lord, you cannot do things out of duty for God, you must do them out of love for God.

In the Book of Nehemiah, we see an amazing, historic, and world changing event unfold. The people of God, after seventy years in captivity in Babylon are back in the promised land, and in particular the city of Jerusalem. They have an assignment from Heaven, to rebuild the nation of God, the city of God, and the Temple of God. It was a great work for a small remnant. The Prophet Jeremiah prophesied the day would come when he wrote, *"For thus says the Lord: After seventy years are completed at Babylon, I will visit you and perform My good word toward you and cause you to return to this place. For I know the thoughts that I think toward you, says the Lord, thoughts of peace and not of evil, to give you a future and a hope. Then you will call upon Me and go and pray to Me, and I will listen to you. And you will seek Me and find Me when you search for Me with all your heart. I will be found by you, says the Lord, and I will bring you back from your captivity" Jeremiah 29:10-14*. The small remnant of God's people had a great destiny. They were to do three great things for God by rebuilding their city and nation, and re-establish the worship of Almighty God in the temple of God. It was a long, grueling journey from Babylon, and when they arrived at Jerusalem, it was a wasteland.

The leaders of the people went right to work when they arrived. Nehemiah and the prophet Ezra were amazing elders who led the people by example. They understood the importance of the great work assigned to them, and they were determined to move on it quickly. As daunting as it was, their rebuild began to take shape. The gates and the walls were rising from seventy years of devastation. It was a monumental undertaking, and the enemies of God's people and God's building project were plentiful and persuasive in the land. *"But it so happened, when Sanballat heard that we were rebuilding the wall, that he was furious and very indignant, and mocked the Jews. And he spoke before his brethren and the army of Samaria, and said, 'What are these feeble Jews doing? Will they fortify themselves? Will they offer sacrifices? Will they complete it in a day? Will they revive the stones from the heaps of rubbish—stones that are burned?' Now Tobiah the Ammonite was beside him, and he said, 'Whatever they build, if even a fox goes up on it, he will break down their stone wall'"* Nehemiah 4:1-3. On and on the discouraging words were hurled at God's people, all intending to create uncertainty in their mind about their purpose and put an end to their great work for God.

Soon, the work of rebuilding the Temple was in danger of getting bogged down. Doubt and fear began to displace hope and purpose. God's beloved people became dispirited, and the work was almost at a standstill. Instead of experiencing joy in doing a great thing for God, they experienced despair. Besides the discouraging voices from their enemies, the people of God were overwhelmed by the reading of the Law of the Lord. Instead of producing joy in them, the Law produce condemnation. They felt they could not fulfill the very thing they were in the land to fulfill, obey the Law and the ordinances of God. Their despair began to manifest the more the Law was read aloud. Not only was the enemy attacking them, they felt God's Law was condemning them. Helplessness and hopelessness were setting in. They lacked the revelation of relational joy with God. They only thought compliance to God and the Law were the way. They thought duty was what pleased God. They felt trapped between condemnation from God and accusation from enemies.

As the people of God listened to the Law being read to them, it says that they began to weep. The more the Law was read, the more discouraged they got. They realized, they could never fulfill the Law of God and it broke their heart. These amazing people had been chosen by God to initiate one of the greatest works in human history. They would rebuild and re-establish the nation God had chosen and prepare the way for the coming Messiah, Jesus Christ. In their discouragement they had lost sight of God's great vision and destiny for them. They had left everything familiar in Babylon and traveled hundreds of miles to relocate their families in the promise land, and now they felt powerless to please God and finish the work. The Bible tells us, *"All the people wept, when they heard the words of the Law."* Their hearts were broken over their own spiritual condition, over their lack of strength, over their nation, and the absence of their true worship of God.

Nehemiah and the Prophet Ezra discerned what was happening and made an important decision. The Bible says, *"Nehemiah, who was the governor, Ezra the priest and scribe, and the Levites who taught the people said to all the people, 'This day is holy to the LORD your God; do not mourn nor weep.' For all the people wept when they heard the words of the Law. Then he said to them, 'Go your way, eat the fat, drink the sweet, and send portions to those for whom nothing is prepared; for this day is holy to our Lord. Do not sorrow, for the joy of the LORD is your strength."* It was a breakthrough moment for the people of God. This was the turning point they so desperately needed. These great teachers and leaders reminded the people that it was not legalism God desired, it was the joy of fellowship with Him, and friendship with each other. It was not just doing work for Him, it was simply enjoying Him. Serving God is indeed a wonderful thing and these brilliant leaders understood that truth, but now a greater revelation was shown to them, the revelation of joy and love for God. The Bible says, *"They understood the words that were declared to them."* As a result, the joy of the Lord became the very things that would propel them to complete the work assigned to them. It was the joy of the Lord that strengthened them spiritually, emotionally, and physically. When the people took time to be refreshed by simply enjoying God and each other, their strength to serve God was renewed!

Discouragement is a real enemy of the people of God. It is an arch enemy of your spiritual life. If you've battled it, you know how powerfully devastating it can be. It will blind you from the things God is doing right in front of you. It is a thief that will steal your time, energy, and future.

Discouragement has a loud voice too. It lies to you about who you are, how God views you, and what others think of you. Its forceful influence can pull you into deception if you have no strength to resist it. Its manipulation has led many astray. It causes weariness and brokenness of mind and can easily wound your soul. Discouragement can break your will to serve God faster than anything you can imagine. If it is left to fester and grow, discouragement will leave you hopeless, helpless and in despair.

Nehemiah reminded the people of God, amid persecution, uncertainty, and hard work that the joy of the Lord must be remembered and embraced. Without it they would have no source of strength for the great work they were doing for God in Jerusalem. It's not the task or the assignment God gives you that empowers you, it's the joy of His grace and love for you that empowers you. Their discouragement was a lie. Their despondency was a deception. Their future was to rebuild a nation of worshippers and rebuild the place of worship and fellowship with God in the earth. They thought God wasn't pleased with them—but, God was pleased with them, and He gave them a revelation that you and I are still strengthened by today. It took discerning and loving leaders to help God's people see that when there is no joy in the heart, there is no strength in the hands. To build anything for God the joy of the Lord is essential.

Beloved, if you desire to do great things for God, you must develop great joy in Him. Your joy in Christ must be equal to the great things He asks you to do for Him. When you serve Him out of the joy in your heart, you will never find yourself under the harsh hand of discouragement again. The fact is God's promise still holds true centuries after the great work of rebuilding the city of God was completed. When you have the joy of the Lord in your heart, you will possess the strength of God for any task in your hands!

Declaration of Joy: "Heavenly Father, thank You for the strength that Your joy gives me! My assignments for You are wonderful, but without Your joy in me I will have no strength to fulfill them. Fill me with Your joy and I shall be filled with Your strength. I rebuke burnout and embrace burning brighter with Your great love. Strengthen my hands and my heart. Strengthen my will and body! Let the strength of Your right Hand be in me. Let my love for You flourish and my joy in Jesus overflow. In the mighty Name of Jesus I pray, Amen!

CHAPTER 14

"JOY AT THE THRONE OF GOD"

"For what is our hope, or joy, or crown of rejoicing? Is it not even you in the presence of our Lord Jesus Christ at His coming? For you are our glory and joy."
I Thessalonians 2:19

You can feel the emotion of the apostle Paul in this verse. Like a window into his soul, the old apostle opens his heart and allows you to gaze into the deep love he has for those he sacrificed so much to reach. In this verse, he discloses something very personal about himself that, so few understand today. And, how can they understand what Paul is revealing if they have never labored in prayer for a lost soul until that soul was gloriously saved? Unfortunately, most church attenders think this type of spiritual labor and love for souls is old-fashion and archaic, but that is far from the truth. This type of care and burden for the lost runs through the deepest parts of the heart of Christ and through all those who walk closely with Him.

Carrying a burden for the lost seems to be scarce these days, even though it need not be at all. It appears too heavy to bear for some and too involved for others, but again it need not look that way to you. The truth is the burden of the Lord for the lost has a simple and sweet blessing of joy associated with it. Both the burden and the blessing are what the Father longs to give to all those who seek to know His heart in this important matter. It's what the apostle Paul spoke of in this verse as he expressed his heart to the Thessalonian church. This burden and blessing are what every child of God should ask the Father to impart to them every day.

When you carry a burden for the lost you carry the very purpose of God in your heart. You grasp the reason why the Father sent the Son. *"For God so loved the world that He gave His only begotten Son, that whoever believes in Him should not perish but have everlasting life. For God did not send His Son into the world to condemn the world, but that the world through Him might be saved" John 3:16-17.* To seek and to save the lost is the highest aim of the Father and the Son and, will be for those who closely follow Christ. Since it was the reason Jesus came and died, it must be the reason you go and tell.

A burden for the lost is not a burden in the natural sense. When you labor before the Lord in prayer, assurance comes from Him that they will be saved. His promise is sure when our prayers are fervent. The Spirit of God comforts you concerning the lost, even when you don't see evidence of change in them. He encourages you and reveals to you, as you labor that they will stand with you one day before His Throne. The apostle Paul makes it unmistakably clear in this verse and in all his epistles, that his greatest joy in life, his most significant eternal reward was that all those he diligently labored to win to Christ would stand blameless before the Lord with him.

Paul's burden and joy worked together within him to bring in the harvest he was sent to reap. When you take up the burden of the Lord for a lifetime, you too will see a bountiful harvest of souls over your lifetime. Paul was a wise master builder for Christ. His burden, his joy, his wisdom, his prayers, his work, his writings, and his relationships all worked together to produce the glorious fruit of souls saved. Proverbs 11:30 says, *"The fruit of the righteous is a tree of life, and he who wins souls is wise.* Will you win souls to Christ? Then, employ the Lord's burden in your heart and the Lord will empower your life with His blessing every day. Rescuing the perishing takes courage, faith, compassion, patience, love and above all else the leading of the Holy Spirit. Since Christ lives in you and you have the mind of Christ, you are more than equipped to win the lost around you. Your burden, along with your readiness in the Spirit to seek and save them will keep you focused and on-target each day.

The world is perishing, and everyone outside of Christ is lost and perishing as well. However, it is not the Father's heart that any should perish, but for all to be saved through repentance and faith in Jesus Christ. It should cause you great concern that your lost loved ones and friends could perish without Christ. I assure you, if you will engage in earnest care for their souls and prayers before the Lord, the Lord's fruitful burden will come upon you. Will you carry His burden for the lost? Unless God's people carry His burden for the lost, so many souls will tragically perish in the flames of hell. Are you willing to carry His burden and enter His harvest? His burden opens the door to the bountiful harvest He desires to reach. In the end, when you stand in the Presence of the Lord with those you helped rescue, you will know the exuberant joy the apostle Paul expressed. *"For what is our hope, or joy, or crown of rejoicing? Is it not even you in the presence of our Lord Jesus Christ at His coming? For you are our glory and joy." I Thessalonians 2:19-20.* The souls you labored for will be like jewels in your crown of rejoicing as you gladly stand in the presence of the Lord Jesus.

If you do not have the burden of the Lord for the lost, let Jesus place it in you. If you have not felt an urgency lately to pray for the lost do not be discouraged. The Lord loves to gently pour His burden into those who are open to Him and to those who will ask Him for it. The apostle Paul was a soul winner. Jesus said, *"Follow Me, and I will make you fishers of men" Matthew 4:19.* That's what developed for Paul, and that's what develops for all those who closely follow Christ. You too will become a fisher of men, a winner of souls, an influencer and persuader of men as you follow Christ. I'm convinced, there's a great soul winner on the inside of every single child of God. All you need to do is ask the Lord for His sweet burden. It will not be long thereafter until you know the great joy of souls coming to Christ. In the end, nothing is of greater importance than souls saved. What a great day that will be when we can say to our friends and loved ones like the old Apostle, *"You are my glory, joy and crown of rejoicing in the presence of the Lord."*

Declaration of Joy: "Thank You, Heavenly Father for the burden to win souls. I gladly receive it and gladly cultivate it. I will not allow the enemy to hinder my love for the lost. Pour into me Your great love for the lost. Let your joy overflow as You gently impart Your heart to win souls into me. Lead me by Your Holy Spirit as I speak to my friends and loved ones about the Gospel. Open their heart as I share with them and pray for them. I will enter Your harvest and win souls for You! I want to stand before You with my loved ones and friends by my side! In the powerful Name of Jesus I pray, Amen!

Conclusion

Following are some more wonderful passages from God's word about the joy of the Lord. I pray that your heart will be continually filled and overflowing with all the fullness of Christ's life-giving joy! I pray this book, in some small way will help lead you into greater spiritual victory, fruitfulness, and fullness in Christ Jesus our Lord.

Bible Verses On The Joy Of The Lord

"Beloved, I pray that you may prosper in all things and be in health, just as your soul prospers. For I rejoiced greatly when brethren came and testified of the truth that is in you, just as you walk in the truth. I have no greater joy than to hear that my children walk in truth."
3 John 1:2-3

"His lord said to him, 'Well done, good and faithful servant; you were faithful over a few things, I will make you ruler over many things. Enter into the joy of your lord.'"
Matthew 25:21

"Blessed are you when men hate you, and when they exclude you, and revile you, and cast out your name as evil, for the Son of Man's sake. Rejoice in that day and leap for joy! For indeed your reward is great in Heaven, for in like manner their fathers did to the prophets."
Luke 6:22-23

"What man of you, having a hundred sheep, if he loses one of them, does not leave the ninety-nine in the wilderness, and go after the one which is lost until he finds it? And when he has found it, he lays it on his shoulders, rejoicing. And when he comes home, he calls together his friends and neighbors, saying to them, 'Rejoice with me, for I have found my sheep which was lost!' I say to you that likewise there will be more joy in heaven over one sinner who repents than over ninety-nine just persons who need no repentance."
Luke 15:4-7

"Now it came to pass, while He blessed them, that He was parted from them and carried up into heaven. And they worshipped Him, and returned to Jerusalem with great joy, and were continually in the temple praising and blessing God. Amen."
Luke 24:51-53

"Therefore, those who were scattered went everywhere preaching the word. Then Philip went down to the city of Samaria and preached Christ to them. And the multitudes with one accord heeded the things spoken by Philip, hearing and seeing the miracles which he did. For unclean spirits, crying with a loud voice, came out of many who were possessed; and many who were paralyzed and lame were healed. And there was great joy in that city.
Acts 8:4-8

"And the word of the Lord was being spread throughout all the region. But the Jews stirred up the devout and prominent women and the chief men of the city, raised up persecution against Paul and Barnabas, and expelled them from their region. But they shook off the dust from their feet against them and came to Iconium. And the disciples were filled with joy and with the Holy Spirit."
Acts 13:49-52

"But none of these things move me; nor do I count my life dear to myself, so that I may finish my race with joy, and the ministry which I received from the Lord Jesus, to testify to the gospel of the grace of God."
Acts 20:24

"Not that we have dominion over your faith but are fellow workers for your joy; for by faith you stand."
II Corinthians 1:24

Moreover, brethren, we make known to you the grace of God bestowed on the churches of Macedonia: That in a great trial of affliction the abundance of their joy and their deep poverty abounded in the riches of their liberality. For I bear witness that according to their ability, yes, and beyond their ability, they were freely willing, imploring us with much urgency that we would receive the gift and the fellowship of the ministering to the saints."
II Corinthians 8:1-4

"I thank my God upon every remembrance of you, always in every prayer of mine making request for you all with joy, for your fellowship in the gospel from the first day until now."
Philippians 1:3-5

"For this reason we also, since the day we heard it, do not cease to pray for you, and to ask that you may be filled with the knowledge of His will in all wisdom and spiritual understanding; that you may walk

worthy of the Lord, fully pleasing Him, being fruitful in every good work and increasing in the knowledge of God; strengthened with all might, according to His glorious power, for all patience and longsuffering with joy; giving thanks to the Father who has qualified us to be partakers of the inheritance of the saints in the light. He has delivered us from the power of darkness and conveyed us into the kingdom of the Son of His love, in whom we have redemption through His blood, the forgiveness of sins."
Colossians 1:9-14

"And you became followers of us and of the Lord, having received the word in much affliction, with joy of the Holy Spirit."
I Thessalonians 1:6

"But do not forget to do good and to share, for with such sacrifices God is well pleased. Obey those who rule over you, and be submissive, for they watch out for your souls, as those who must give account. Let them do so with joy and not with grief, for that would be unprofitable for you."
Hebrews 13:16-18

"Therefore if there is any consolation in Christ, if any comfort of love, if any fellowship of the Spirit, if any affection and mercy, fulfill my joy by being like-minded, having the same love, being of one accord, of one mind. Let nothing be done through selfish ambition or conceit, but in lowliness of mind let each esteem others better than himself. Let each of you look out not only for his own interests, but also for the interests of others."
Philippians 2:1-4

"Thank you for taking time to read my book on the joy of the Lord. I trust it has enriched your walk with Christ and has given you a revelation of His grace and power that will take your spiritual life to new heights."

I would so appreciate it if you would take a few moments of your time today to write a review of my book on Amazon. Your review will help create more interest in this book, encourage others to purchase, and read it for themselves.

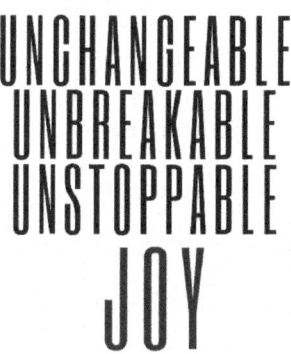

Living a life of triumph and joy
RANDY D. RICE

If you live in the Cincinnati area, I would love for you to attend one of our Sunday morning worship services at the church I pastor, LifeChurch West Chester. You can go to lifechurchwestchester.com to watch our livestream and watch previous sermons and series by clicking the media tab.

You can also checkout out The Prophetic Pulse Podcast and YouTube channel where me and my associate, Pastor Curtis Hill dive into discussions on the critical issues facing Christians today. Find us on Youtube, Facebook, and wherever you get your podcasts.

Again, thank you for reading the book and getting to know me better and our LifeChurch family. I look forward to meeting you soon and encouraging you continually in your walk with God!